Julain's Jottings

Poems and Writings By

Julain Krahn

Mill Lake Books

Mill Lake Books
Chilliwack, BC, Canada
https://jamescoggins.wordpress.com/mill-lake-
books/

Cover design by Dean Tjepkema

ISBN 978-1-998787-00-5

About The Author

Writing for enjoyment and fun.

For Julain it has been a wonderful way to express herself. Starting around age 9, she would write out her thoughts. She also played piano, flute, and enjoyed playing with the family St. Bernard dog, Taco, and Smokey our Siamese cat.

Life was busy but there was always time for writing in her early years.

Thank you, Julain, for sharing them with us.

Love,

Your family

Acknowledgment

Thank you to

Ryan Krahn and Jason Krahn (Julain's nephews)

for typing out the poems

and for helping to edit them.

"The Lord is my shepherd. "

Psalm 23:1

Fun - Jottings

Glasses

There once was a rabbit or hare,

Who hopped up and down, here and there,

It was clear as could be,

He needed glasses to see,

For he ran into things everywhere.

Pumpkins

pumpkins;
in the garden
everywhere,
some even stare!
delicious pies
for everyone,
and a happy birthday
for my mom!

Love Julain

Pumpkins

Pumpkins in the garden

Everywhere,

Some even stare!

Delicious pies for everyone,

And a happy birthday

For my Mom!

Love Julain

A Seed

Once when I planted a seed,

It got strangled by a mean old weed.

I chopped the weed up

And put it in a cup,

And felt I had done a very good deed.

Salmon

There once was a salmon in the sea,

Who swam when a worm he did see,

But the worm had a hook

So, the fish turned his look

And let the poor little worm be.

Ideas

Put the pen to paper

When the head is full of

Expressible ideas.

Maybe some lofty

New solution to

My head

Will appear.

The Little Things

The little things

A look, a smile,

A quiet word,

A listening ear,

Caring,

Sharing,

They may seem small,

But to me,

The little things,

Mean the most of all.

Talk

There is a time for silence and a time for talk.

Where talk tires your tongue,

Silence can be a wonderfully refreshing experience.

Nowhere in the Bible does it say we must talk.

New Boots

New boots look great,

But inside are hard and uncomfortable.

Sort of a feeling of status

That only lasts a short time,

But to have this status

We must pay an uncomfortable price.

Until the sole conforms to the feet,

And the boots

Slowly become air conditioned.

While the status goes down,

The comfort goes up

And once again,

It's time to buy

New boots.

Boring

There once was a karate class so boring,

So consequently, it caused much snoring.

The plot was right,The student was bright,

But the mix for that age was deploring.

Lies

They're uttered so very easily,

At an unexpected time.

It doesn't hit your conscience,

It doesn't seem a crime.

Then suddenly you realize,

That what you've said is not true

And now you're really sorry

That you did not think it through.

You ask for the forgiveness

Of everyone who heard,

Now all has been forgotten

Of those distorted words.

Summer

Birds wheeling
Overhead
Crying
Their complaints
Of no food.
Kids lie
On the beaches
To
Burn their
Skin
And shrivel
Up.
Nobody worries
About homework
Everybody plays and nobody
Works!

The sun beats
Overhead
And heats the
Earth
Until it burns
Our
Feet.
Ah! Summer.

Snow

Again, comes the snow

A common friend, somewhat comforting,

Drizzling, it goes on endlessly...

And for a time, the world we know

Becomes beautiful and glorious.

What a pretty existence we know!

For even after the snow departs,

In the air lingers a mist,

A scent of the oncoming age.

What else to look forward to?

But again, will come a time... wherein

We will call out for the snow

And it will come again.

A common friend, somewhat comforting.

The Eagle

The eagle

Flying, soaring, like the wind,

He's a spirit

Called upon by nature.

He knows no master,

Only freedom.

I see him one day,

Call out to him.

Wishing I could be him.

The wind

Is my only master.

Housework

The water isn't running,

The fridge isn't humming.

The oven isn't heating,

The beater isn't beating.

My coffee isn't perking,

I'm all that's still working!

The Song of Forever

The song came drifting into my mind,

Where it tumbled and tossed throughout the night.

It ended my fears, and helped me to find

A peace and a calm which I might

Not have reached, even though it was not

By chance that it found me,

Such a song; many, many times,

And not found it.

Those times, it had found me,

But I stopped it

So foolishly, I see at last.

This time though, was different.

The change was not in the song,

So, it must have been in me.

The next morning, I woke up, frantically

Searching for the song,

Which I thought was lost, since I couldn't quite
remember it.

Patiently waiting for me to sing it once more,

Forevermore

Friends – Jottings

Friends

Caring, loving

Listen, comfort, understand

Friends are yours forever

'togetherness'

My Friend

In all my life, I must confess

No others have I known,

Whose affections, goals, and daily cares

Have matched so close my own.

You and I are friends it's true,

And yes, we sometimes part.

But their friendship does find a way

To join our yearning hearts.

Though beauty I behold in you

It's all the eye can see.

I value as much the inner you

For all eternity.

I promise not what I can't give,

And I say this in truth

We'll be friends till time runs out,

Of this my heart's the proof.

We've come so far and shared so much,

Perhaps then, dreams come true.

For all my life I've dreamt of love

In the friend I've found in you.

True Friends

You are a true friend,

You understand and are patient,

I can count on you being to the end.

When things don't go quite the way I'd like,

You share my tears and help carry my burdens.

Your love seems to cover all my fears.

I know that I am not alone.

You share with me all my joy, and even talk about boys,

We can laugh and be just plain silly,

Thank you for accepting me just the way I am.

Keep laughing, your smile brightens my day.

You are open and honest, yet kind,

You bring out the true feeling inside me.

All of my weaknesses you seem to find. I have nothing to hide.

All the while you are building me up.

I need your encouragement,

Especially when I feel like a helpless little pup.

You are unique and special, thank you for being part of my life.

A friend like you deserves the highest medal.

I hope I can be all that you are to me.

The Value of a Smile

It costs nothing but creates so much.

It enriches those who receive, without impoverishing those who give.

It happens in a flash and the memory of it sometimes lasts forever.

It creates happiness in the home, fosters goodwill in a business and is the countersign of friends.

It is rest to the weary, daylight to the discouraged, sunshine to the sad and nature's best antidote for trouble.

Yet it cannot be bought, begged, borrowed, or stolen for it is something that is no earthly good to anybody till it is given away!

Goodbye to a Friend

Now that you're leaving, I feel that

I've taken you for granted.

All those little things you did for me seem

To take on a new meaning,

And I wish I could carve them into my mind forever
but at the time, they seemed so trivial.

Now I suffer.

I'm so glad we've become close friends.

You were always there when I needed a reassuring
hug or some soft-spoken words of wisdom.

I will always remember that voice; it will play like a
record through my mind.

I'm comforted that God's hand is on your life,
guiding you, protecting you, using you.

How I've grown closer to Him because of you!

I thank God for the gift of your friendship, praying
that I've enriched your life as you have mine.

And although we have diverged into our own
separate lives, we will always be friends because
special things never lose their value.

Friends

Forever

Dedicated to Marilyn, her baby, and family

Her laughter lingers in the night air.
Her eyes twinkling with a love for life and people.
It is her time, young and pretty.
Enjoying all the things a twenty-three-year-old
should.
A diamond ring on her finger, a husband, the first
baby soon.
Going out to celebrate these occasions.
She thought she would make it. "23"
Such a wonderful celebration, surrounded by the
ones she loves, and love her---husband, parents,
family. All so happy.
Worrying thoughts, sudden terror, fears ending in
tragedy.
An innocent victim of our insane, senseless world.
One fall turns a day of life into a nightmare of grief
and sorrow for parents who loved their child, a
brother, left heart broken, and a husband who
watched her go.
But why? What purpose is there? And what about
me? I am almost "23", I have a family, boyfriend,
friends. I am filled with fear, rage, sorrow, trying to
imagine being a part of her family and loved ones.
She will never have her baby, have a career and
watch her children grow up.
All things I want and plan to do someday.
She thought she would make it. "23"
Lord, you say you have a purpose, and I believe you
do; so, I pray that I can say I will always look to you
like Marilyn did.
This girl that I admired was loved by many, Lord.

I pray that you will be with us and let us know your love.
Lord, even though I am so young, help me to realize; I have to make sure each day counts. But I know God's hand is on me, I know He will always be beside me, and though I love this life He is giving, if I went now, I know I would keep on living.

All my love and more,

Julain

Loneliness

No smiling or laughing

There is no fun anywhere,

Being alone hurts.

The Light

But to be a candle that shines very bright.

Let them know about your best Friend,

In Him they will find friendship that will never end.

Think Of Me

Think of me...
When others have gone,
When times get tough
And you are all alone.

Think of me...
When skies turn grey,
When confusion sets in
And friends turn away.

Think of me...
As day slips to night,
Trying to believe
Things will work out right.

Think of me...
When the wind blows cold,
Makes you lonely
Let's emotions unfold.

Think of me...
As time flies by,
When things don't work out and you want to cry.

Think of me...
When things go right,
I look up, I trust that you might.

Think of me...
There's no need to prove-
Just let your thoughts
Of me, be filled with love.

Love as an Evergreen Tree

To many people,
Love is symbolized by a rose.
With understanding that-
A rose is beautiful and bright,
With a sweet fragrant smell
It seems so peaceful.

But a rose does not last.
As hard weather arises,
It's colour and smell fades,
The leaves die and wither leaving behind
An unattractive stem, and,
If you get too close you get pricked.
To me,
Love is symbolized by an evergreen tree.
It may not look or smell like a rose.
But it is strong and sturdy,
Ready to defend-
Against anything.

And it lasts.
Harsh weather may come,
But my tree stands firm.
It even provides shelter with its outspread
branches.
It blocks pollution,
Taking it upon himself so I won't suffer.
To me.
Love is an evergreen tree.

The Cry

Why is it that we,
When we feel something there
And want to share it, Can't.

We often think that they
Will hear our thoughts, but
Not understanding, Laugh.

It happened before
And we recoiled in shame,
But tried again Yet failed.

The pressure is too much.
Can't handle it alone,
Withdraw inside and cry.

They leave us alone,
Seen as an outcast,
And the Desperation grows.

One day in a crowd
We hear of One who cares,
Who'll take our hand, who'll love.

We fall on our knees
Knowing our hearts are exposed,
Accept and receive Christ.

We see others there-
As we were; they're searching,
And now we do share
Him!

LIFE

A home of the lonely, a haven for the lost,

A cry of desperation, another war fought.

An Island of prosperity, a sea of poverty,

A land of interest, a place of monotony.

A glimmer of hope, a shadow of fear,

Seldom a smile, more often a tear.

An entity of cliffs, a series of valleys,

High steep roads, short narrow alleys.

Clouds of blessings, thundering hardships,

Calm relaxed faces, hard snarling lips.

A friendly word, a warm, firm hug,

A slap in the face, shoulders that shrug.

A flower of joy, A growing of excitement,

A curtain of sorrow, many enticements.

A cushion for the weary, the land for the brave,

A whirlwind of fury, serious, quiet, grave.

A circle of hate, a river of love,

A light in the darkness,

That comes from above!

Sometimes I Wonder

Sometimes I wonder

How it would be,

If I were a string of spaghetti

Instead of me.

Would I just be cooked?

In an old pot?

Or would I mold?

And turn noses a lot?

Would I be a tasty meal

In someone's tummy?

Or would I feel

When he burps and says, "yummy"?

Again, would I just turn soggy

Of water being boiled?

And turn me straight

From once been coiled.

Sometimes I wonder

How it would be,

If I were a string of spaghetti

Instead of me.

Snoopie

Little cuddly kittens,

Snuggle in your lap.

They love it if you comb them

While they take a nap.

Little snuggly puppies

Like to go for walks,

But sometimes they are very bad,

So, you have to give them talks.

Happy Prayers

Sometimes I feel lonely,

Sometimes I feel grey,

So, when I really need a friend,

I just sit alone and pray.

The World

The world is huge; but yet so small.
Hanging in a space almost ready to fall.

How strange it looks, circling around that turning
sun.
Twisting, turning, and having fun.

But take a closer look, what is within?
Wants and sadness are caving it in.

Then what can they do, the human race,
To make the world a better place?

Love, faith, and trust in God's love,
Will bring the world together like a glowing white
dove.

Family – Jottings

Families

Families are important,

They hand out love and care.

Home is where we learn,

Especially to share.

They also help us listen,

And teach us to be fair.

They often share out hugs and kisses,

When I have had a nightmare.

That is why families are important,

To not have one is rare.

Home

It's nice to travel

Far and near,

With things to do

And sounds to hear

But no matter

Where you roam,

There's no place

As nice as home.

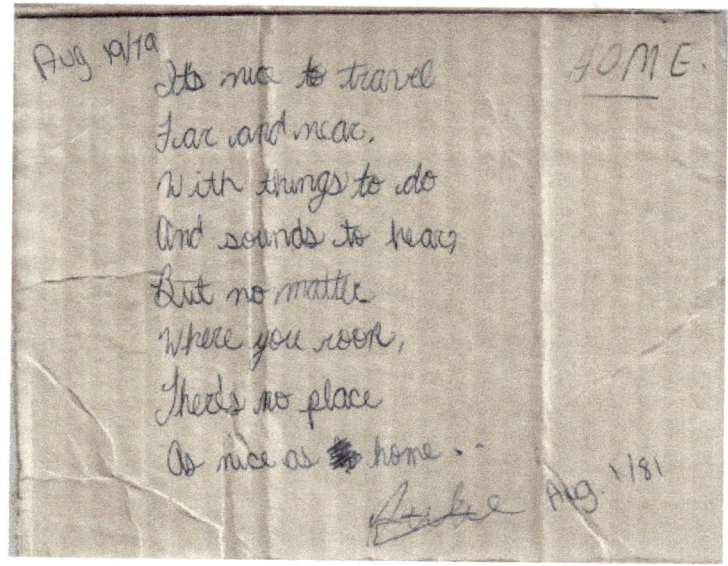

My Family

My Mom is my mentor,

My confident, my guide.

She's always there to help me,

She never leaves my side.

My Father is my role model,

My discipliner, my friend.

When something goes wrong,

His help he will lend.

My brothers are my playmates,

My best friends and more.

Even through our hard times,

My Family is my solid rock,

My strength, and my tree.

They help me to grow; and they're

What make me, me.

Burned

I have a family who has been burned.

I thought by now they would have learned.

They go in the sun,

And when they're all done,

Some real nice red bodies they have earned.

Yes, Friends, You Only Make Me Smile

My two big brothers are David and Jon

We're the kids of Mr. And Mrs. Krahn

They treat me real nice and all love me

Maybe I've matured? So, I'm more set free

Well, my life is more rearranged now

And just because all my friends have changed wow

So, I won't hurt my family anymore

That's because God has opened a love door

I've always thought it's just I'm getting old

It's more I've grabbed a mind and found gold

I almost hope this life never ends

Just because now my family are my friends.

My Mom

You are a true friend,
You understand and are patient.
I can count on you being
There to the end,
When things don't go quite the
Way I'd like.

You share my tears
And help carry my burdens,
Your love seems to cover all of
My fears.
I know that I am not alone.

You share with me all of my joys,
We can laugh and be just plain old silly
And even talk about 'boys'.
Keep laughing, your smile
Brightens my day.

You are open and honest, yet kind,
You bring out the true feelings
Inside me.
All of my weaknesses you seem
To find; I have nothing to hide.

All the while you are building
Me up.
I need your encouragement,
Especially when I feel like
A helpless little 'pup'.
Thank you for accepting me
The way I am.

You are unique and special,

Thank you for being part
Of my life.
A Mom like you deserves
The highest medal.
I hope that I can be
All that you are to me.

Dearest Mom

I hope you remember to make toasted muffins

and eggs for breakfast tomorrow.

Have a nice day

Julie

Mom, My Best Friend

What could I ever have done to deserve your friendship?

When no one else is near, you are always by my side

Before I can even begin to understand the complex burdens of my heart

You already know just where the trouble lies

There is something I will never grasp

But you consistently understand

You take me away to a quiet peace and place

And open my blind eyes from your perspective

I'm in your Master Plan.

What could I have done to deserve your friendship?

Nothing.

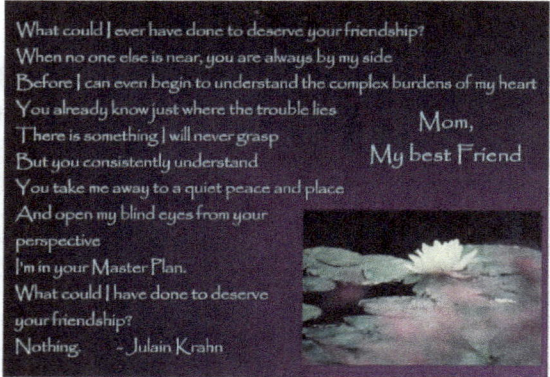

34

Mom, My Best Friend (Original)

What could I ever have done to deserve your friendship?

When no one else is near, you are always by my side. Before I can tell you the troubles of my heart you already know where the burdens lie.

There is something I will never grasp, but you have unfailing understanding.

When I am bothered, your love takes me to a quiet tranquil place and opens my eyes to see things from your perspective.

Thank you for accepting me as part of your family. During happy Times you send me a smile of delight. I am grateful for every blessing, big or small.

I will never comprehend your devotion to me; but I know this; it will last a lifetime.

You and I have gone through rough and dangerous times, thank you for setting me down to stand up straight when the fierce storms have passed us by.

I lean on you for strength and peace of mind, I can face each day with a smile, knowing you are here for me.

What could I have ever done to deserve a mother like you?

Nothing.

What is a Mother?

A mother can be any size or any age, but she won't admit to anything over 30.

A mother has soft hands and smells good.

A mother likes new dresses, music, a clean house, her children's kisses, an automatic washer, and Daddy.

A mother doesn't like having her children sick, muddy feet, temper tantrums, loud noise, or bad report cards.

A mother can read a thermometer and like magic, kiss a hurt away.

A mother can bake good cookies and pies but likes to see her children eat vegetables.

A mother can stuff a fat baby into a snow suit in seconds and kiss sad little faces and make them smile.

A mother is underpaid, has long hours, and gets very little rest.

She worries too much about her children, but she says she doesn't mind at all and no matter how old her children are, she still likes to think of them as her babies.

She is the guardian angel of the family, the queen, the tender hand of love. A mother is the best friend anyone ever has.

A mother is love!

Dear Dad

I just wanted to tell you some of the things

that I appreciate about you.

You play games with me, family is most important

to you, you play catch with me, you take me to

hockey games and we cheer for the Canucks, you

are my hero, you are a very respected man, takes

me to the Sizzler and eats the steak so I can have

the all you can eat shrimp, has been married to my

Mom for over 36 years, tries to protect me from all

my loser boyfriends, does not charge me a lot for

rent, lets me eat hamburgers without the patty.

Dear Dad, The Difference We Can Make

Sun rises, sun sets,

Have I made a difference yet?

Going to work, enriching my mind,

Going home to do work which has been assigned.

We really are selfish you know,

We don't think of others who feel low,

I'm not helping anyone,

If I'm not proclaiming God's son.

Lord, today I pray,

I can be a blessing in some little way.

Why are we here? Is a question we must ask,

In order to find our own special task.

Living in circles with nothing to do,

Is something that hurts others too,

Look in God's word and you will find,

Words that will help you slowly unwind,

Remember God loves you,

Remember to love him too,

Because of everything He has done for you.

Dear Dad,   The Difference We Can Make

Sun rises, sun sets;
Have I made a difference yet?
Going to work, enriching my mind,
Going home to do work which has been assigned.
We really are selfish you know
We don't think of others who feel low;
I'm not helping anyone,
If I'm not proclaiming God's son.
Lord, today I pray,
I can be a blessing in some little way.
Why are we here? Is a question we must ask,
In order to find our own special task.
Living in circles with nothing to do,
Is something that hurts others too,
Look in God's word and you will find,
Words that will help you slowly unwind
Remember god loves you,
Remember to love him too.
Because of everything He has done for you.

Love, Julain

Fathers

Fathers are important,

They hand out love and care;

Home is where we learn,

Especially to share;

They also help us listen,

And teach us to be fair;

They often share out hugs and kisses,

When I've had a nightmare;

That's why fathers are important,

To not have one is rare.

39

My Dearest Dad

Your knowledge oh Dad

Is shown through your wisdom.

You gave me the gift of life

For which I can never repay you.

Your love for me I cannot entirely grasp,

You know me and yet still love me for who I am.

Oh Dad, what have I done for you?

Take my life and teach me to be like you,

That I may show others your wonderful nature.

Silent Cries

Dad, you somehow know me,

I mean really know me;

Sometimes I do not want you to discern

My unhappy thoughts.

So, I plaster on a smile and hope my fears are
secured and that nobody will see them.

The aching inner me you somehow acknowledge.

Everybody else is too caught up in themselves,

They do not hear my inexpressible cries.

I love you Dad.

2 friends +2 gether = 4 ever

Dad part 1

You may have thought I did not see
Or that I had not heard
Life's lessons that you taught to me
But I got every word.

Perhaps you thought I missed it all
And that we would grow apart
But Dad, I picked up everything
It's written on my heart.

Without you, Dad, I would not be
The woman I am today
You built a strong foundation
No one can take that away.

I've grown up with your values
And I'm very glad I did
So, here's to you Dear father
From your forever grateful kid.

Dad part 2

You are my hero, Dad

You're my secure foundation

When I think of you, I'm filled with love

And fond appreciation.

You make me feel protected

I'm sheltered by your care

You're always my true friend and Dad

Wher I need you – you are always there.

You have a place of honour

Deep within my heart

You've been my superhero Dad

Right from the very start.

I Can Dream

I can dream...

I can believe... same as the abutting person,

But when God does not seem to help me through,

I will not leave everything to live

Around the burned-out shell of a dream.

I will look for tangibility and security

And leave the cinders of the dream behind.

Then... He overtakes me,

There are no rigid words or protests of
disappointment,

I hear only expressions of understanding.

He has given me time... as if He had

All the time in the world

To love me...

To walk with me...

To make my dreams come true...

I can dream...

For dreams are goals, based on hope and faith...

I can believe...

For together, God and I can reach any dream...

If I use the time He gives me...If I am patient with
His plan...

If I find reality in Him...I can dream.

The Wake of the Waves

Swish, swish, swish, as they roll towards caves.

To the shore they roll relentlessly on course.

Relentlessly racing to break with great force.

So powerful are they that they conquer the seas.

Often preying on people disregarding their pleas.

King of the sea as they oft' have been called.

Yet how gentle are they, and how beautiful when
sprawled.

A friend to the shore as it caresses the sand.

Like the warmth of the sun as it tempers the land.

A beautiful gift from the Heavens above,

Which is ruled by God's Mighty Love.

Birthdays

Again, comes the birthday

A common friend, somewhat comforting

Haunting, it goes on endlessly...

And for a time, this year we know

Becomes bright and glorious.

What a super existence we know!

For even after the birthday departs,

In the air lingers a memory,

A scent of the oncoming age.

What else to look forward to?

But again, will come a time... wherein

You will receive another birthday

And it will come again.

A common friend, somewhat comforting...

Love in July

July,
A time when the earth blooms,
And clothes herself
On magical fields
Of flowers and life.
July,
The month when
Love appears,
Dancing in the violets, and
Racing through fields
Of golden wheats.
It plays beautiful music
Among the lovers,
And even surprises
The unsuspecting,
Its glory can't
Be hidden.
Gleaming cover
This emotion man's strongest
Will not be concealed,
July is the month when
The earth awakens
After her long slumber,
And love inhabits her
Once again.

Together We Will

Admire what is beautiful.
Desire what is passionate.
Sing what is lovely.
Speak what is sweet.
Dream what is colourful.
Caress what is soft.
Shed a tear for what is sad.
Experience what is perfect.
Create what is memorable.
Respect what is true.
Be thankful for what is natural.
Hope for what is possible.
Depend on what is dependable.
Laugh for what is joyful.
Encourage what is best.
Pray for what is wise.
Adjust to what is new.
Admire what is carefree.
Understand what is comprehensible.
Respond to what is respondable.
Enjoy what is good.
Fulfil what is meant to be.
Prefer what is of good judgement.
Care for what is humble.
Appreciate what is attempted.
Compliment what is deserving.
Need what is necessary.
Strive for what is challenging.
Love what is loveable.
Wonder what is Godly.
Imagine what is wholesome.
Live what is proper.
... as one.

Without Your Love

I am helpless without your love,

even if I have all the Queen's treasures.

I am alone if your love is not by my side.

You will never know how much I think of you

and how much I love you.

I try to thank you,

but the words get in the way.

Faith – Jottings

New Life in Heaven

Every day's a new day to be found,

With joy as we know where we're bound,

To heaven's great plain

Where people remain,

As glorious lights who are crowned.

Our Pastor

Pastor Warren,

Our Pastor is bright and unboring.

Talking about The Light, so we'll listen

And won't all be snoring.

In Him

Every person has had a friend,

But not everyone has The Friend.

Some know the privilege exists,

But others still remain in the dark.

We are vessels of Him,

And the signs who point to Him.

It is the actions we display,

That may bring one more Friendless home.

It is our duty not to hide the Light,

But to be a candle that shines very bright.

Let them know about your best Friend,

In Him they find friendship that will never end.

In Him

Every person has had a friend;
But, not every one has The Friend.
Some know the privilege exists;
But others still remain in the dark.

We are vessels of Him,
& the signs who point to Him.
It is the actions we display,
That may bring one more Friendless home.

It is our duty not to hide the Light,
But to be a candle that shines very bright.
Let them know about your best Friend,
In Him they find friendship that will never end.

- Julain Krahn

WHAT DO YOU THINK?

55

Healing Hurts

I pick my way through
Problems of this world.

I shudder at the
Pain.
(Who will push the button?)
What is hope?

I stare at the
Distended bellies.
Why no food?

I weep at the
Piles of murdered
Babies.
(It could have been me.)

I accuse
God.
Where is Your love?

He reminds me that the
Hurts
Are man-made on earth.

I can only
Wait
For you to open up your
Heart,
And let God's
Love
Heal the
Hurts.

Healing Hurts

I pick my way
Through
Problems
Of this world.

I shudder at the
Pain.
(Who will push the button?)
What is hope?

I stare at the
Distended bellies.
Why no food?

I weep at the
Piles of murdered
Babies.
(It could have been me.)

I accuse
God.
Where is Your love?

He reminds me that the
Hurts
Are man-made on earth.

I can only
Wait
For you to open up your
Heart,
And let God's
Love
Heal the
Hurts.

– JuLain Krahn

WHAT DO YOU THINK?

In the Beginning

In the beginning God Created the heavens and the

earth and all that is therein.

To us he gave it for our enjoyment.

We cover the earth with asphalt roads and parking

lots,

stab the sky with concrete and glass structures

obscure the sky, deaden the air with pollution.

We engross ourselves with the affairs of our

existence

seldom taking time to enjoy Nature, one of God's

many gifts,

About which we seldom think and even take for

granted.

Go and see such a place not so marred by

"civilization".

Go and see what God has made for us.

In the heart of undisturbed wilderness.

Where serenity reigns

There are innumerable things to experience.

The sunshine bravely chasing night away

as the sun peeks over a mountain.

The sun, a violent inferno of incandescent gases full

of warmth, yet it sustains life here.

The flowers yawning turn and face it smiling,

brightening with their colours

The grassy meadows swaying in the zephyr and

gently rustling.

The warm cool breeze is sweet and fresh

And higher up, the wind Plays and tumbles in the

puffy bubbly cumulus clouds

Of fair weather coaxing them along through the

expansive sea of sky

which perfectly fades of opalescent blue,

From light to dark in the zenith

In a perfect blend unmatched by any artist.

As the sun rises from the horizon of the sky

it's rays send from the clouds,

Shadows tracing patterns on the ground and

nearby hills

Covered with trees

Whose many coloured leaves of green, yellow,

orange,

brown flutter by the breeze on their branches

And coat the forest floor.

The sun, past its greatest height

Leaves begins to descend.

Darker clouds creep up stealthily

and obscure.

A rain drop falls, then another and another.

Rain begins to fall quenching the earth's

thirst more and more,

but then recedes

as the sun beams back on earth

Pouring forth its light.

The clouds lie

and in their wake

tug a rainbow,

Most glorious in beauty,

a bright shining arc of shimmering luminescence

God's signature of His everlasting promise.

The sun sinks lower

Its reflection dancing joyfully on the ripples of the

lake fed by rivers rushing.

From the mountains a soul soothing sound.

Evening draws nigh,

And soon the moon,

Earth's younger brother,

But cousin to the sun

Slowly rises

As the sun sets in a resplendent display of color,

Trimming cotton clouds in silver-gold.

Embracing the moon, the stars twinkle and sparkle

like

Diamonds

Like they did

In the beginning when God

Created nature

For our enjoyment

Because He loved us.

Tribute to My God

God you're the greatest!
You
In Your infinite wisdom created Me!
Planned and designed me
To Your exact specifications.

You sat down
And made a map of my life.
One that would give me everything that I needed
And one that would make me
Happiest and most fulfilled.

But You also left room on this map for
My wrong choices – and bad decisions.
You made enough detours and bridges
So, I could travel back
To Your road at any time.

And this You did
For every person that ever lived,
Or ever will.

God, I can see You in these
And it increases my wonder
And total amazement at Your creativity,
Unchanging wisdom
And awesome love for mere humans,
Just like me!

Thanksgiving Celebration

Tribute to My God

God you're the greatest!
You
In Your infinite wisdom created Me!
Planned & designed me
To Your exact specifications.

You sat down
And made a map of my life.
One that would give me everything that I needed
And one that would make me
Happiest and most fulfilled.

But You also left room on this map for
My wrong choices—and bad decisions.
You made enough detours and bridges
So I could travel back
To Your road at any time

And this You did
For every person that ever lived,
Or ever will.

God I can see You in these
And it increases my wonder
Anc total amazement at Your creativity,
Unchanging wisdom
And awesome love for mere humans,
Just like me!

WHAT DO YOU THINK?

- Julain Krahn

Dear Lord

Your beauty oh Lord

Is shown through your Creation.

You gave us the gift of life

For which we can never repay you.

Your love for us we will never comprehend.

For when we sinned, you died that we might live,

That we could be cleansed and saved from eternal death.

We fail you constantly

And yet you forgive, and are constantly faithful to us.

Oh Lord, how much you have done for me and what have I done for you?

Take my life and make me a servant

That I might show others your wonderful love.

Thank you

Thank you for the steps we take

Thank you for the friends we make

Thank you for the games we play

Thank you for this sunny day.

Thank You Jesus

Thank you Jesus

For my Father who loves me

For my Grandfather who prays for me

And for God my eternal Father

Who made me and is always with me

How blessed I am

Amen

Amen

Thank you for our home so dear

Thank you for the clothes we wear

Thank you for the toys and for the sand

Thank you for God for Father's hand

Amen

Help My Lord

I'm lost in darkness; all alone,

Conformed to this world, I'm just a slug.

Some people laugh at me and some people cry,

But me, I might as well just die.

Now I stand, I'm so confused,

I have to win, I cannot lose.

I feel like going somewhere to cry,

Don't ask me questions; I can't say why.

I dreamt a dream or so I thought,

And realized love takes quite a lot.

But now it's gone. Or did it come?

It matters not, all is done.

Help me Lord, before I drop,

Heal the pain, make it stop.

Help me Lord, make me new,

Teach me to love, love like You.

Thank you, God,

Thank you, God, for making the earth,

Thank you for the chance of a second birth,

Thank you, God, for all your love

From your home in heaven above.

Thank you for forgiving my sin,

Thank you, God, for letting me in,

Thank you, God, for making me,

Thank you, God, for not leaving me.

Thankyou God   By Julain
                                    Krahn

Thankyou God for making the earth,
Thankyou for the chance of a second birth,
Thankyou God for all your love
From your home in heaven above.

Thankyou for forgiving my sin,
Thankyou God for letting me in,
Thankyou God for making me
Thankyou God for not leaving me

The Reason for the Season

The Lord is my Christmas,

I look through Him to see

Christmas in a slightly different light

in a better perspective.

The Lord alters my view on the earthly Christmas

and because He is the reason for the season,

I see things clearer

than I ever could on my own.

My Lord protects me from rains of sorrow,

The angry winds, and the cold of loneliness;

Yet lets the Son shine through

Giving all His warmth and comfort.

My every purpose is the Lord

but can be abused, hurt or misused

by Satan, the world or me.

But can also be repaired if damaged,

by simple, sincere words of prayer.

My spirit can always be cleaned again,

the dust and dirt of sin wiped away

by the cleanser of souls.

My God, the Window

My Lord is a window,

I look through Him to see

the world in a slightly different way,

a different light.

He alters my view of earthly circumstances

And though He is the pane of glass

Between me and the world,

I see things clearer

than I ever could on my own.

He protects me from the rains of sorrow,

the angry winds, and the cold of loneliness,

Yet lets the Son shine through

In all His warmth and comfort.

This shield that is my Lord

Can easily be broken, or shatter, or dirtied,

by Satan, the world and me.

But, it can be repaired if damaged, by the simple,
sincere words of prayer.

It can always be cleaned again,

the dust of sin wiped away

by the cleanser of souls.

The Change in Me Is You

Without your love in me here,

I merely exist.

With your love existing in my soul,

My senses sparkle.

You make me appreciate,

The essence of all creations.

You make me notice,

The security your love brings.

Every Day

Finish every day and be done with it.

Some blunders.

Tomorrow is a new day.

With God's help.

"And I shall dwell in the house of the Lord forever."

Psalm 23:6

More About the Author

Julain would grow her hair and then donate it so that the hair could be made into wigs for those that needed it.

Julian went to great lengths to help a child.

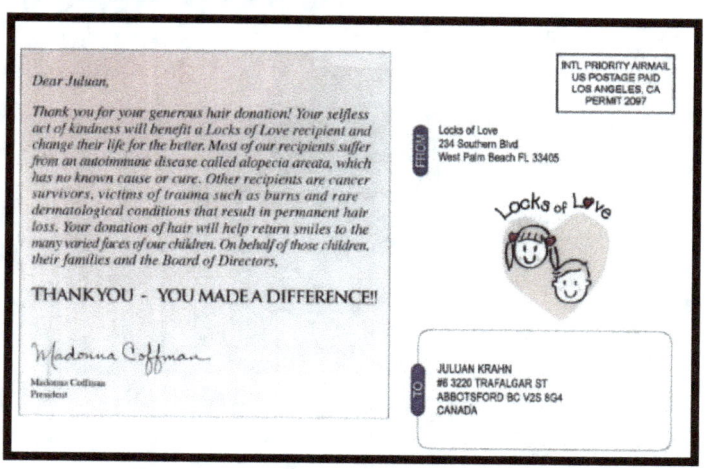

Julain also enjoyed hand painting dishes, assembling puzzles and making Gingerbread houses.